LOOK AND SAY

WHAT YOU SEE AT THE SEASIDE

D1429635

To Catherine, who loves the seaside
and especially the puffins!

S.B.

First published in 2019 by Nosy Crow Ltd
The Crow's Nest, 14 Baden Place, Crosby Row
London SE1 1YW
www.nosycrow.com

ISBN 978 1 78800 250 9

'The National Trust' and the oak leaf logo are registered trademarks of The National Trust (Enterprises) Limited (a subsidiary of The National Trust for Places of Historic Interest or Natural Beauty, Registered Charity Number 205846).

Nosy Crow and associated logos are trademarks and/or registered trademarks of Nosy Crow Ltd (Registered Company Number 7130282).

Text © Nosy Crow 2019
Illustrations © Sebastien Braun 2019

The right of Nosy Crow to be identified as the author and Sebastien Braun to be identified as the illustrator of this work has been asserted.

All rights reserved

This book is sold subject to the condition that it shall not, by way of trade or otherwise, be lent, hired out or otherwise circulated in any form of binding or cover other than that in which it is published. No part of this publication may be reproduced, stored in a retrieval system, or transmitted in any form or by any means (electronic, mechanical, photocopying, recording or otherwise) without the prior written permission of Nosy Crow Ltd.

A CIP catalogue record for this book is available from the British Library.

Printed in China

Papers used by Nosy Crow are made from wood grown in sustainable forests.

1 3 5 7 9 8 6 4 2

LOOK AND SAY

WHAT YOU SEE AT THE SEASIDE

Sebastien Braun

nosy crow

Have you ever been to the seaside? There's usually a lot to see and it's especially great if you can visit when the sun is shining.

Can you see . . . ?

ice cream

kite

deckchair

umbrella

What do you like
to do at the beach?
beach ball
picnic
suncream
sun hat
dog

The beach is the perfect place to practise building sandcastles.

Can you see . . . ?

seaweed

bucket

spade

fossil

You can decorate them with things
that you find washed up on the shore.

sandcastle seashell driftwood feather pebbles

Look at all the people splashing around in the water!
Can you see . . . ?
rubber ring
turnstone
armbands
razor shell

Some are using snorkels so they can breathe underwater!
sanderling
snorkel
surfer
lifeguard
mermaid's purse

It's busy by the harbour with boats sailing in and out. There are a lot of hungry seagulls, too.

Can you see . . . ?

yacht

lighthouse

fishing rod

seagull

bench

dinghy

speedboat

porpoise

cat

From the top of the cliffs, there's a great view of the seaside below. It's often very windy, so hold on to your hat!

The paraglider loves the wind as it takes him flying over the sea.

Can you see . . . ?

tree

kayak

tern

cave

signpost
sheep
paraglider
climber
kittiwake

The rock pools are full of animals.
Some are bright and colourful,
but some blend in to the rocks
and don't look like animals at all!

Can you see . . . ?

sea anemone

shore crab

prawn

sea urchin

You have to look closely
to see the world underwater.
mussels
whelk
limpets
periwinkle
hermit crab

Further out at sea, fishing boats are catching fish. It can be slippery on deck – especially when there's a storm.

Can you see . . . ?

fishing net

seal pup

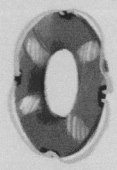

lifebelt

wellington boot

How many seals can you count on the rocks?
buoy
albatross
flag
lobster pot
seal

An estuary is where a river meets the sea and they're brilliant places to go birdwatching.

Can you see . . . ?

heron

curlew

oystercatcher

lapwing

Most birds that live here have long legs for wading in the water.
otter
reeds
dragonfly
coot
caterpillar

Sand dunes are big hills of sand and you'll often find them at the seaside.
Can you see . . . ?
butterfly
buzzard
beetle
stoat

Lifeguards
If you look closely, you might see a lot of tiny animals hiding in the sand.
spider
bee
grass snake
sand lizard
rabbit

Many animals live completely under the water, so they spend all their time swimming. Some have special gills to help them breathe.

Can you see . . . ?

dolphin

whale

basking shark

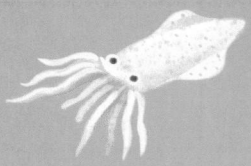

squid

How many legs does the octopus have?
jellyfish
scuba diver
sponge
eel
octopus

Some creatures even live right at the bottom of the sea. Can you see any animals that are shaped like stars?

Can you see . . . ?

coral

lobster

blenny

stickleback

Coral might look like a plant, but it's actually an animal, too!
cuttlefish
starfish
anchor
seahorse
flatfish

Sometimes around the coast you'll see high walls of rock called cliffs.

Can you see . . . ?

puffin

nest

chick

egg

Some birds make their nests on the clifftops – it can be very noisy and smelly!
thistle
thrift
cormorant
gannet
gorse